DIARY OF A MAD STOCK TRADER OR 50 SHADES OF PLAY

Hugh McDowell

© May 2015

I'm going to level with you right up front. I am a stock trading junkie! I love matching wits with the stock market. I love short term trades that don't take much research, time or capital.

There's nothing quite like it when at the end of the day the play you've made is the only trade on that stock for the day.

You have used your judgment to place a trade that no one else has made. Depending on the outcome you are either a genius or an idiot. Sometimes you're the hammer, sometimes the nail.

What a rush when you're the hammer. Not so much when you're the nail.

Of course many times you aren't the only one making a particular trade on a stock. I write a blog to that effect called Beatthemarketwithhugh.wordpress.com.

The contents of this book are 50 trades that I've made in the last two and a half years. Most are option plays but there also stocks bought and sold as well as covered call plays.

The most current trade ended April 24, 2015. The earliest trade I've listed ends August 13, 2013. The first eleven trades were made in April and March of this year (2015). The first twenty one trades are all from January 2015 to April 2015. These are current trades not something from seven or eight years ago. I may add more trades prior to finishing this book. Depends on how fast I type and what the market offers.

I'm not talking about huge amounts of capital. My money at risk from a single trade has ranged from a low of $30.64 to a high of $605.63. Most fall somewhere in-between. And the majority of these 50 trades involved less than 30 minutes of research.

All of my research is free provided that one has access to the internet.

I've been playing the market for over 15 years. For more information about me check out my website: www.neweraprojects.com. You can also go to www.amazon.com. Type in my name, Hugh McDowell and the books and reports I've written on playing the market will pop up.

When you look at these trades make sure to examine the rate of return percentage. The average savings account in a bank returns less than 2% annually. More on the annual rate of return calculations in a bit.

I intentionally play single option trades to prove a point. You don't need a huge amount of capital to play the market. What you will need when you actually start trading is a discount broker. The commissions and fees of a full service broker are way too expensive for single option trades.

As you review the trades, think about playing with more capital or trading more than one option. Your net gain and rate of return can increase substantially playing multiple options. Of course the risk is greater.

In one sense I am a lazy trader. I don't want to spend hours of time or huge amounts of capital on my trades. I like quick turnarounds. The markets today are so volatile that I don't like to tie up my money for any great length of time.

Often I will go days or weeks without even looking at the market. Then I may turn around and make trades three or four days in a row.

Sometimes if I have only 20 spare minutes when the market is open I will quickly check it out. I've made trades at the market open, a few hours into the day and fifteen minutes prior to market close.

It all depends on my schedule. My point is that you don't need to spend hours on a daily basis watching the market. Unless you want to!!!

I can't remember the last time I sat for hours watching the market. It isn't necessary.

Anyone can learn to trade like I do. You can also adapt these trading strategies into long term investing. Just takes a different mindset and some variations on your trading parameters.

I've kept this report free of charts. I want to show the mechanics of the trades.

For the first 25 trades I give an overview of the transaction. I explain how I found the stock, why I chose to play it, market conditions and the amount of research I had to do. For trades 26-50 I just give the transaction with no description. If you want to read 25 more stock trade descriptions you're more of junkie than I am! Lol.

You will see both winning and losing stock trades. Some of the stocks I play are well known (MSFT, SBUX, GMCR, YELP). Others are relatively unheard of (VNCE, VEEV, NES, FINL). My trading strategy doesn't depend on any specific category or type of stock.

Here are a couple of points for clarification.

In my stock trade descriptions often they will be in both present and past tense grammatically. This is because some are copied just how I wrote them on the day I played them. Other descriptions have been edited for clarity, sometimes days or weeks after the fact. This doesn't affect the content of the message in any way.

When I mention market or markets I am referring to the Dow, the S&P and the Nasdaq.

Let me go through one of the trades I've listed. I will explain how to read the header categories as well as how I calculated the rate of return and the projected annual rate of returns on these trades. It may seem complicated but it's really quite simple. All I use is a simple calculator for the calculations.

Let's start with the very first trade I have listed here. The ticker symbol is UCTT. The very first thing you see is the ticker symbol for the stock and the actual date I initiated a play.

Directly beneath this are the transaction details. Date tabs are the dates I bought and sold the option or stock. Activity tab describes the buy or sell action. The Qnty/Symbol tab show the amount of options or shares, the stock symbol and whether the trade involves a call, put or stock. The Description tab tells the option expiration date and the strike price. If there is just a stock play there will be the number of shares bought or sold. The price tab is what I paid for the option or the stock. The Fees tab is the broker fees for the trade. The Amount tab is the total result of the transaction.

The next line shows the amount of money risked on the transaction, the net gain or loss and rate of return percentage as well as the number of days to complete the transaction.

To get the rate of return you take the net gain and divide it by the money at risk. For UCTT it goes like this. 23.71 divided by 85.35 = 27.779%. The amount is usually a little higher but I stop at three numbers past the decimal.

The annual rate of return is a projected rate. Here's how I calculated the annual rate of return. There are 365 days in a year. Divide 365 by the amount of days in the rate of return. In this example 365 divided by 4 = 91.25. Always round down to a whole number, in this case it would be 91. This means that if you traded every four days for 1 year you could trade 91 times. Multiply 91 times the rate of return. For UCTT this would be 91 x 27.688. The result is 2,527.889%.

Some of the projected annual rates of return are phenomenal, especially the two day trades. I get lightheaded thinking about it!

Let's get started.

UCTT- April 21, 2015

Date:	Activity	Qnty/Symbol	Description	Price	Fees	Amount
4-21-15	Bot to Open	1 UCTT call	Jun 19 5.00 call	$0.80	5.63	$85.63
4-24-15	Sold to Close	1 UCTT call	Jun 19 5.00 call	$1.15	5.65	$109.34

Money at risk: $85.35   Net gain: $23.71   Rate of Return: 27.779% in 4 days

ANNUAL RATE OF RETURN: 2,527.889%

This quick trade was low risk with high percentage return potential.

Tuesday, April 21, 2015.

The markets were mixed this morning. The Dow and the S&P were down slightly and the Nasd was up slightly.

Sporadic morning for me. Been away from the computer several times this morning. Got back to look at the market four hours into the trading day.

I found UCTT on the Yahoo loser list. The stock had hit its 52 week low at $5.26.

Brand new stock for me, I had never heard of it. The stock was down due to poor guidance for Q2.

Trading volume for the stock was huge. Over 1.7 million shares traded, over 10 times the average.

I spent about 15 minutes researching the stock. I liked both the May and June 5.00 call plays.

So I did something I seldom do. I placed bids for both the May 5.00 call and the June 5.00 call.

I bid .50 for the May 5.00 call. The bid/ask was .50/.80.

I then bid .75 for the June 5.00 call. The bid/ask was .75/.85.

Neither filled in the first 10 minutes. I decided to raise my bid for the Jun 5 call to .80. It filled immediately. I cancelled my May 5.00 bid.

I would have been happy filling either bid but my preference was the June call. This gives me more time to realize a profit for a slightly larger amount of capital.

I expect the stock to recover this week or next, enough for me to see a profit.

Friday, April 24, 2015

The markets are all in positive territory this morning. It's about an hour since the market opened. I just turned on the computer and saw that UCTT was $6.13, up 47 cents.

The bid/ask for my May 5.00 call was .95/1.35. That's a wide spread for a lower priced stock. I put a sell order in for $1.15 and it sold immediately. Alright!

An additional kick for me is that one and a half hours into the trading day, I have the only sale of that option. That will probably change before the day ends but I love matching wits against the market and making over 27% in four days. No one else in the world has done that with this stock at this moment in time.

My prediction on how this stock would perform was spot on. I could have waited since I have until June 19th until the option expires. But I like trading, I don't like holding positions over the weekend and the high rate of return in a short time was too hard to pass up.

NTES- April 17, 2015

Date:	Activity	Qnty/Symbol	Description	Price	Fees	Amount
4-17-15	Bot to Open	1 NTES call	May 15 110.00 call	$6.00	5.63	$605.63
4-20-15	Sold to Close	1 NTES call	May 15 110.00 call	$6.75	5.66	$669.34

Money at risk: $605.63   Net gain: $63.71   Rate of Return: 10.519% in 4 days

ANNUAL RATE OF RETURN: 957.229%

This is a stock that I have played several times in these 50 trades. Risky and highly volatile, it has the potential for very good returns.

Friday, April 17, 2015

Markets down big this morning. I had a chance to check out the market about an hour into the trading day.

One of my stock portfolios showed NTES at $112.28, down $3.96. This is a highly volatile stock that I have played before. A check on the NTES historical price page showed that on April 10, 2015 the stock price was $120.00. Just one week ago.

I decided to bid for a May 110 call for $6.00. The bid/ask at the time was 5.80/6.50. It filled within five minutes as the stock continued to drop.

There was no news specific to NTES. I think it is following its volatile pattern. Another factor in the drop was that it was following in concert with the overall drop in the market today.

My expectation is that next week it will swing back up enough for me to see a decent profit.

Not a lot of research necessary as I am familiar with NTES. Nothing I can do now but wait. My bid filled four hours into the trading day. I'll be away from my computer until after the market closes.

This is the most I have paid for an option in these 50 trades. It is a bigger risk than I normally take but since I've played NTES before, it's a risk I'm willing to assume.

Monday, April 20, 2015

The markets opened in positive territory. I happened to be up early today and checked the market 17 minutes after the open. NTES was up about a dollar.

The bid/ask on my May 110 call was 6.40/7.30. I placed a sell order for $6.60 and it sold immediately for $6.75! Hooray!!!

This was a nice return for 2 trading days. I had the weekend to wait it out. And at the end of the day I checked on Yahoo for the number of these options traded. Mine was the only one. Imagine that, in all the world only I sold that particular option and made a profit on it today.

Now that's a rush.

NSAM- April 15, 2015

Date:	Activity	Qnty/Symbol	Description		Price	Fees	Amount
4-15-15	Bot to Open	1 NSAM call	May 15	20.00 call	$1.10	5.63	$115.63
4-16-15	Sold to Close	1 NSAM call	May 15	20.00 call	$1.30	5.65	$124.35

Money at risk: $115.63   Net gain: $8.72   Rate of Return: 7.541% in 2 days

ANNUAL RATE OF RETURN: 1,372.462%

This trade surprised me with its quick turn around.

Wednesday, April 15, 2015. TAX DAY!

About an hour into the trading day the markets were all in positive territory. On the Yahoo loser list I found NSAM, an asset management company.

The stock was $19.51, down $2.94. New company to me, I had never seen it before.

There was no news at this point to say why the stock was trading lower. The trading volume was huge, over 9 million shares traded in less than an hour. Average trading volume for NSAM was 1.3 million.

A look at the historical price list for NSAM showed that the stock had not traded below $20.00 for several months.

I bid for a May 20 call for $1.10. The bid/ask at the time was .90/1.40. My order filled almost immediately.

My total research time on this stock was 10 minutes.

I'm not sure why there is such high trading volume with no news.

A few minutes later a news item popped up. The stock had spiked up the day before at the end of the trading session. I imagine today's selloff was some profit taking.

In the next 30 days I expect the stock to go high enough for me to see a profit. My total cost and money at risk is $115.63

Thursday, April 16, 2015

Markets are down slightly today. I didn't even check the market until 2 hours after the opening bell.

NSAM was up about 40 cents from yesterday. My May 20 call option bid/ask was 1.10/1.30. I put a sell order in at $1.30.

I didn't think that it would sell. If it did, I would make a small two day profit.

The option doesn't expire until May 15, 2015 and I expect NSAM to rise in price.

I had to leave for the rest of the day and I didn't get back until 2 hours after market close.

I was surprised to see that my NSAM sell order had been executed. My research and order time for the two days was less than 25 minutes.

Heck, if I could make 7.541% every two trading days I would be thrilled.

SBUX- April 9, 2015

Date:	Activity	Qnty/Symbol	Description	Price	Fees	Amount
4-09-15	Bot to Open	1 SBUX call	May 15 47.50 call	$1.38	5.63	$143.63
4-10-15	Sold to Close	1 SBUX call	May 15 47.50 call	$1.80	5.65	$174.35

Money at risk: $143.63   Net gain: $30.72   Rate of Return: 21.388% in 2 days

ANNUAL RATE OF RETURN: 3,892.616%

This is how you want your option trades to work.

On Thursday, April 9, 2015 the markets all were down a little in the morning. In one of my stock portfolios I saw that SBUX was down to $47.73. It was over $90.00 per share the day before. What the heck?

Turns out the stock did a 2 for 1 split. Often a stock split is good news for the stock and the investors.

I've followed SBUX for years. Traded it as well. The market had been open for 2 hours. I placed a bid for a May 47.5 call for $1.38. The bid/ask at the time was 1.38/1.42. My order filled within minutes.

I expect to see a quick profit on this trade. At this price level more investors and institutions will be adding SBUX to their portfolios. As a result the stock should go up.

Also, an overall up day in the market should help raise SBUX stock price.

I could have bought an April call option but wanted the extra time with the May call option. Just in case the play went the wrong way.

Since I was familiar with SBUX I didn't need to spend a lot of time on research. For this trade I spent about 15 minutes prior to placing the trade.

Friday, April 10, 2015

The market opened in positive territory. I didn't look at the market until it had been open for about two and a half hours.

SBUX performed as I had expected. The price was only up 33 cents but that allowed me to sell my call option for a 21.388% return in 2 days. Not bad.

Of course I could have waited. The option doesn't expire for another 31 days and there is a good chance SBUX will continue to go up. But anytime I can get over a 20% gain in two days I usually take it.

I don't like to hold trades over the weekend when you can get this type of return. Too much can happen in the world that could affect my play in the wrong direction.

MSFT- March 28, 2015

Date:	Activity	Qnty/Symbol	Description		Price	Fees	Amount
1-28-15	Bot to Open	1 MSFT call	Feb 20	42.00 call	$0.88	5.63	$93.63
2-04-15	Sold to Close	1 MSFT call	Feb 20	42.00 call	$0.55	5.65	$49.35

Money at risk: $93.63   Net loss: $44.28   Rate of Return: (47.292) % in 8 days

This iconic company should have made me a decent profit. I was too quick to pull the trigger.

MSFT January 28, 2015

I took a large percentage loss on this trade but the money at risk was small. My reasoning was right on the money and if I had waited closer to the expiration date I would have made a decent profit.

All markets down big today. I had watched MSFT drop yesterday, from $47 down to $42. It was down another 62 cents when I decided to try an option play.

I bid for a Feb 42 call for 0.88. The bid/ask at the time was .88/.89. This was about 2 hours into the trading day. It filled almost immediately.

There was no really bad news specific to MSFT. The big fall (from my perspective) was that APPL had come out strong with a great earnings report.

One analyst wrote that MSFT's "problems included an unexpectedly soggy PC market after a buying rush sparked by the end of Windows XP, an ongoing dip in companies' spending on Office software, problems in Japan and China and a strong U.S. dollar eating away at the value of its huge overseas revenues."

It seemed to me to be an overreaction. The stock price is as low as it has been in several months.

My expectation is that the stock will recover enough in the next few weeks for me to see a profit on the option play.

My total capital at risk is $93.63

I would expect with a large up day in the market and investors deciding to purchase MSFT at this level the stock should pop up.

2-14-15

MSFT price has stayed flat since I bought the call option. I was sure the stock was going up but one of my trading rules is to exit a trade with a 50% loss if the play goes the wrong way.

So I sold the option today for a loss. That still gives me half of the capital from this trade to work with.

2-20-15

Today the stock price ended at $44.15. I would have been able to sell my option for at least $225.00.

I don't like to lose on a trade but no reason to beat myself up over it. You can't always time your trades correctly. I've found it better to set trading parameters and stick with them.

GMCR- March 26, 2015

Date:	Activity	Qnty/Symbol	Description	Price	Fees	Amount
3-26-15	Bot to Open	1 GMCR call	Apr 17 115.00 call	$3.40	5.63	$345.63
4-08-15	Sold to Close	1 GMCR call	Apr 17 115.00 call	$3.65	5.65	$359.35

Money at risk: $345.63   Net gain: $13.72   Rate of Return: 3.969% in 14 days

ANNUAL RATE OF RETURN: 103.194%

Market continued its down trend.

GMCR (Green Mountain Coffee Roaster) is a company I've watched before. I may have played it a year or so ago. Its downtrend continued from yesterday.

The stock today was $114.63, down $3.07. Yesterday it had dropped $6.00.

This stock has wild swings in price. A quick look at the historical price page showed that the last time the stock was near this low was February 5, 2015. The price then was $115.30.

I didn't see any major news why the stock was dropping so much.

The market had been open for about 2 hours. The trading volume for GMCR was not huge.

I looked at some April 115 calls. The bid/ask was 3.20/3.40. I placed a buy order for $3.40 and it filled immediately.

I could have bid lower but I decided I definitely wanted to buy the option. I knew that by placing my bid at the ask price I would get it.

The option expires April 17, 2015. I anticipate with an overall up day in the market the stock should go up.

Also, with such a drop in the last two days I expect buyers to come back in.

Research was about 10 minutes but as I mentioned, I was somewhat familiar with the stock and its trading patterns.

April 8, 2015

After buying the call, GMCR went lower for several days and then flattened out. When the stock hit $118.00 today I decided to sell for a small profit. No need to keep waiting for the stock to have a dramatic increase.

To be fair, I expected the stock to bounce higher than it did. When the trade stopped moving in the direction I wanted it was time to exit.

April 17, 2015

The stock never got above $115.00 today. Had I held the option this long I would have lost my total $345.63 investment.

DSKY- March 16, 2015

Date:	Activity	Qnty/Symbol	Description	Price	Fees	Amount
3-16-15	Bot to Open	1 DSKY call	Apr 17 7.50 call	$1.40	5.63	$145.63
4-09-15	Sold to Close	1 DSKY call	Apr 17 7.50 call	$1.59	5.65	$153.35

Money at risk: $145.63   Net gain: $7.72   Rate of Return: 5.301% in 25 days

ANNUAL RATE OF RETURN: 74.214%

Another unknown stock that made me a small profit.

Monday, March 16, 2015

US markets were up big today. On the Yahoo loser list I found DSKY, a Chinese gaming company.

The stock was $8.36, down $2.46. The company reported a significant decline in revenue expectation. A little over two hours into the trading day the trading volume on the stock was huge. Over 1.2 million shares had been traded. Average trading volume is less than 450,000.

I spent about 15 minutes of research on the stock, all from the Yahoo finance page.

Chinese companies can often be tricky beasts to play. They can be very volatile with big price swings on a day to day basis.

I wasn't familiar with the stock but thought that the market had overreacted and that the stock was oversold.

The stock seemed to be stabilizing around $8.46. I placed a bid for an Apr 7.50 call. The bid/ask at the time was 1.35/1.70 and my bid was for $1.40. It filled immediately.

I think the stock will gain back some of its loss prior to the April option expiration date. I have 33 days before the option expires.

Thursday, April 9, 2015.

The markets opened in negative territory but with an hour to go before closing had moved into positive territory.

It took this long for my DSKY option to finally realize a profit. The option still has another week before it expires but I'm not comfortable waiting so close to expiration. Yeah, it might go higher but it might go lower. I'll take the 5.301% gain.

In all honesty, I thought I would see a larger profit and much sooner. But after purchasing the option the stock went lower, then flat, then finally back up.

I'm satisfied with the gain but certainly not ecstatic.

VNCE- March 19, 2015

Date:	Activity	Qnty/Symbol	Description	Price	Fees	Amount
3-19-15	Bot to Open	1 VNCE call	Apr 17 17.50 call	$1.15	5.63	$120.63
3-31-15	Sold to Close	1 VNCE call	Apr 17 17.50 call	$1.30	5.65	$124.35

Money at risk: $120.63   Net gain: $3.72   Rate of Return: 3.083% in 13 days

ANNUAL RATE OF RETURN: 86.324%

Another small profit made, but I sold too soon. Would have made monster gain had I waited.

Thursday, March 19, 2015

I didn't look at the market until 25 minutes before it closed. Both the Dow and the S&P were down and the Nasd was up. The Dow was down triple digits.

I quickly glanced through the Yahoo loser list and found VNCE. This is a retail clothing company that beat its Q4 profit forecast but had lowered its 2016 revenue forecast.

The stock was $17.84, down $3.55. It had also hit its 52 week low today. The trading volume was over 3 million, ten times more than its average volume.

The stock had been trading all day and seemed to stabilize near $17.84.

I think this is way oversold. The market often overreacts on perceived negative news on a stock. And for me, the announcement seemed mixed, beating forecasts but lowering guidance.

About 12 minutes prior to market close I bid for an Apr 17.5 call for $1.10. The bid/ask at the time was 1.10/1.15. I watched for a couple of minutes and decided to raise my offer. I changed it to $1.15. The bid/ask was still 1.10/1.15 and it filled immediately. This was 8 minutes before the market closed.

Tuesday, March 31, 2015

After buying the call option the stock went down and then stayed flat. Not until today did it start to go up. About one and a half hours prior to market close the stock popped up to $18.60. I decided to sell for a small profit and look for another trade. Sixteen days still remain until the option expires but I don't want to risk it going down again.

Turns out I should have waited. On Friday, April 10, 2015 the stock was $20.09. I could have sold my call option for at least $220.00, probably $250.00. Ah well, in a baseball analogy I took a single instead of a homerun!

NTES- March 12, 2015

Date:	Activity	Qnty/Symbol	Description	Price	Fees	Amount
3-12-15	Bot to Open	1 NTES call	Apr 17 100.00 call	$2.05	5.63	$210.63
3-13-15	Sold to Close	1 NTES call	Apr 17 100.00 call	$5.65	5.66	$254.35

Money at risk: $210.63   Net gain: $43.72   Rate of Return: 20.756% in 2 days

ANNUAL RATE OF RETURN: 3,777.592%

This is the second trade of NTES in two weeks. The first is described after this one. Don't be afraid to play a stock over and over if you are familiar with its trading parameters.

Thursday, March 12, 2015

The market was in positive territory today. NTES was down under $97.00 yesterday. Today it dropped to $94.78. The stock's pattern has been to bounce up when it goes under $100.00.

NTES options are pricey. I would have loved to do a March play but the options expire next week. This is too short a time frame in case the trade goes the wrong way.

I decided to go out to April and play a $100 April call option. I placed a buy order for $2.05. The bid/ask at the time was 1.80/2.15.

With about two hours remaining prior to the market close my order filled.

I anticipate that NTES will have its customary upswing.

Not a lot of research for this trade, I was familiar with NTES. Maybe 10 minutes.

Friday, March 13, 2015

Friday the 13th, look out! The markets opened in negative territory and ended the day lower.

About 5 hours into the trading day, NTES was at $96.32, up $1.55 from yesterday. The bid/ask on my April call option was 2.35/2.75. I placed a sell order for the option for $2.60. The order was executed and I was out with a great two day profit.

I could have waited as the option doesn't expire for another 35 days. I was certain that the stock would go higher prior to April 17 but it was a Friday, my return for two days was almost 21% and now I had all my capital plus profit to trade again.

With a larger bankroll I could have afforded to wait longer on this trade. But since I like to play I need capital to make my trades.

On a side note, on April 9, 2015 NTES reached $120.00. Damn, I would have crushed it!

ZGNX- March 11, 2015

Date:	Activity	Qnty/Symbol	Description	Price	Fees	Amount
3-11-15	Bot to Open	100 ZGNX	ZGNX 100 shares	$1.20	5.95	$125.95
3-17-15	Sold to Close	100 ZGNX	ZGNX 100 shares	$1.3501	5.98	$129.03

Money at risk: $125.95   Net gain: $3.08   Rate of Return: 2.445% in 7 days

ANNUAL RATE OF RETURN: 127.14%

On this play I was hoping to buy 100 shares of the stock and then sell a covered call. Didn't go as planned.

Wednesday, March 11, 2015

Markets down slightly today. On the Yahoo loser list I found ZGNX. The stock price was $1.20, down 47 cents. I was surprised to see a stock such a low price selling options. I had never heard of the stock before, it was brand new to me.

The market had been open for about three and a half hours. I spent about 20 minutes doing research on the company, all on Yahoo. The 52 week low for the stock was $1.07 and the 52 week high was $3.98. The stock had reported a larger than expected loss (by 3 cents).

I put a bid in for 100 shares at $1.20 per share. The order filled in 10 minutes. My total cost was $125.95.

Here's my thinking. Since the stock is near its 52 week low if might bounce up enough to see a profit just from buying and selling the stock. And with a total cost of less than $126.00 the risk for me was minimal.

What I want to do is sell an option on the stock, preferably a March call option. The March call options had strike prices of $1.00, $2.00 and $3.00.

I placed an offer to sell to open one March 1.00 call for 65 cents. Had the order filled I would have made a little over 26% return.

The order did not fill.

I have a lot of choices with this play. I own 100 shares of stock, free and clear. I can wait for the stock price to go up and then sell a covered call option. My preference would be to play a short term option but I have the choice to go out to April, July, October or further.

However, if you've read my blog (beatthemarketwithhugh.wordpress.com) or website (www.neweraprojects.com) you know I prefer short term trading.

As it turned out, the stock stayed flat for the next week so I sold the stock for a small profit.

VEEV- March 4, 2015

Date:	Activity	Qnty/Symbol	Description	Price	Fees	Amount
3-04-15	Bot to Open	1 VEEV call	Apr 17 26.00 call	$1.15	5.63	$120.63
3-17-15	Sold to Close	1 VEEV call	Apr 17 26.00 call	$2.00	5.65	$194.35

Money at risk: $120.63   Net gain: $73.72   Rate of Return: 61.112% in 14 days

ANNUAL RATE OF RETURN: 1,588.912%

This was a great result with an unknown stock.

Wednesday, March 4, 2015

Markets all in negative territory this morning. I checked the Yahoo loser list and found VEEV, a stock I've never seen before. This is a technology stock in the healthcare info services industry.

It had beat earnings but was down on buyout talks. The earnings announcement was yesterday and almost 5 hours into the trading day the stock was at $25.44, down $7.25.

Five hours into the trading day the stock price seemed to stabilize between $25-$26. Over 12 million shares had traded so far with the average number of shares traded not quite 1 million.

I thought the market had overreacted and that the stock was near its low for the day.

I placed a bid for an April 26 call for $1.15. The bid/ask at the time was 1.15/1/30. The stock dropped a bit more and my order filled within 10 minutes.

The shorter term March call option was too risky for me. I knew virtually nothing about the stock and wanted give myself more time to see a profit. Total research time was about 20 minutes.

Tuesday, March 17, 2015

For the next week and a half, VEEV stayed flat. Today the stock bounced up like I had anticipated it would. I had gotten up late that morning and five hours into the trading day the stock price was $27.38.

I immediately put a sell order in for $2.00. The bid/ask at the time was 2.00/2.20. It filled immediately and I made a great profit.

I could have waited as the option expiration date is April 17. But over 61% return was too hard to resist.

Geez, if I could make over 61% on my trades every 14 days I would think I had died and gone to Wall Street Heaven! The projected annual return is outrageous!

NTES- February 27, 2015

Date:	Activity	Qnty/Symbol	Description		Price	Fees	Amount
2-27-15	Bot to Open	1 NTES call	Mar 20	100.00 call	$3.40	5.63	$345.63
3-05-15	Sold to Close	1 NTES call	Mar 20	100.00 call	$3.60	5.65	$354.35

Money at risk: $345.63   Net gain: $8.72   Rate of Return: 2.522% in 7 days

ANNUAL RATE OF RETURN: 131.144%

Another NTES trade. High risk for a small gain.

Friday, February 27, 2015

The markets were in negative territory all day and ended the day in negative territory.

NTES is a Chinese gaming stock that I have played before. It is a highly volatile stock with wild price swings up and down.

At one point today the stock had dropped over $6.00, down to $98.84. I had been watching the stock for several days. I wanted to do an option play but had to be careful. NTES options are pricey (for me) and I could lose a significant amount of my capital if I picked the wrong side of a trade.

I had noticed before that when the stock price drops below $100.00, it has a tendency to bounce back up again. This is called a resistance point. A quick look at the historical price page for NTES showed that about two weeks ago the price was over $112.00.

I decided to play a short term, high risk play. When the stock price was $99.76 (down $4.98) I placed a bid for a March 2015 100 call for $3.40. The bid/ask at the time was 3.30/3.60. This was about two and a half hours after the market had opened.

My order filled within ten minutes.

I will need to watch this closely. I expect a bounce on Monday. If the stock price goes the wrong way I could lose a large portion of my investment capital. The option expires March 20, 2015.

Thursday, March 5, 2015

NTES dropped on Monday and Tuesday. So did my stomach! I breathed a sigh of relief when the price started to go up yesterday. Today the stock was up over $4.00 at one point.

I can't afford to wait. My time frame is short and I have a lot of capital tied up in this trade.

I put a sell order in for $3.60. The bid/ask at the time was 3.30/4.00

I checked back about an hour and a half later and the option had sold. This was forty five minutes prior to market close.

I made a small profit and preserved my trading capital.

I will continue to monitor NTES and play it when it meets my trading parameters.

IQNT- February 26, 2015

Date:	Activity	Qnty/Symbol	Description	Price	Fees	Amount
2-26-15	Bot to Open	1 IQNT call	Mar 20 15.00 call	$0.45	5.63	$50.63
3-04-15	Sold to Close	1 IQNT call	Mar 20 15.00 call	$0.75	5.65	$69.35

Money at risk: $50.63   Net gain: $18.72   Rate of Return: 36.974% in 7 days

ANNUAL RATE OF RETURN: 1,922.2648%

Another trade with an unknown stock for a great return.

Thursday, February 26, 2015

Markets are mixed today. Down and S&P down slightly, the Nasd up slightly.

I only had about forty minutes to look at the market today. I haven't played or watched in a couple of days.

I went to my go to strategy. I looked at the Yahoo loser list and found IQNT. The stock was $14.66, down $2.94.

It had reported better than expected earnings and revenue prior to the market open. The trading volume was almost three times its average. I could find no news as to why the stock had taken a hit.

This was about four hours into the trading day. Often when a stock makes a big move up or down early in the day, the price will stabilize within a few hours.

I decided to play a short term trade. I bid for a March 15 call for 45 cents. The bid/ask at the time was .40/.55.

The stock continued to drop and my order filled within a couple of minutes. The option expires March 20, 2015. This gives me 22 days to see a profit. My expectation is that the stock will recover prior to the expiration date.

Wednesday, March 4, 2015

IQNT had started to recover a little during the last two days. Today when it hit $14.96 I was able to sell the call option for a decent profit.

I could have waited longer since the option expires March 20, 2015. But an almost 40% return on my money in seven days was too good to pass up.

My original thoughts on the stock and the play were correct.

This was a fairly safe play without a huge amount of risk.

By the way, I spent less than thirty minutes of research on the stock prior to placing the buy order.

GTS- February 19, 2015

Date:	Activity	Qnty/Symbol	Description	Price	Fees	Amount

| 2-19-15 | Bot to Open | 1 GTS call | Apr 17 | 20.00 call | $1.75 | 5.63 | $180.63 |
| 3-20-15 | Sold to Close | 1 GTS call | Apr 17 | 20.00 call | $1.43 | 5.65 | $143.35 |

Money at risk: $180.63   Net loss: ($37.28)   Rate of Return: (20.638%) in 30 days

My own stupid mistake cost me on this trade. Sometimes you can be doing too much at once.

Thursday, February 19, 2015

Mixed market today. Dow and S&P down slightly but the Nasd is up slightly.

I found GTS on the Yahoo loser list. The stock was $20.65, down $3.47. GTS had reported earnings prior to the markets opening. A health company in Puerto Rico, the report obviously didn't sit well with the analysts.

The sell off seemed like an overreaction to me. I spent about 20 minutes researching the stock. I decided to bid on an April 20 call. Since the stock was totally new to me I wanted some additional time for my play to work.

I bid for an Apr 20 call for $1.75. The bid/ask spread was very large. At the time it was 1.40/2.30. The order filled in about 30 minutes.

My expectation is that the stock will recover prior to the April expiration date and allow me to see a profit.

Frday, March 20, 2015.

Major screw up today. I was doing too many things this morning and sold the option by mistake for a loss.

I thought I was selling for a profit but had mixed up the buy and sell amounts.

Always check and recheck your numbers. Even when you do you will sometimes make a mistake.

I hate it when this happens but such is the nature of being human.

Sometimes you can trade so much that you lose track of the action.

All part of being a mad stock trader!

YELP- February 6, 2015

Date:	Activity	Qnty/Symbol	Description		Price	Fees	Amount
2-06-15	Bot to Open	1 YELP call	Feb 20	45.00 call	$2.25	5.63	$230.63
2-13-15	Sold to Close	1 YELP call	Feb 20	45.00 call	$2.70	5.65	$264.34

Money at risk: $230.63   Net gain: $33.71   Rate of Return: 14.616% in 8 days

ANNUAL RATE OF RETURN: 657.72%

An uncomfortable trade where I broke one of my trading rules.

On Friday, Feb 6, 2015 the market opened in positive territory but ended the day negative. I found YELP on the Yahoo loser list. At $46.35 it was down $11.12. This was an hour into the trading day.

I had heard of YELP but never had looked at the stock. I thought I would try a short term play. I bid for a Feb 46 call for $2.25. The bid/ask at the time was 2.10/2.40. The bid filled shortly thereafter and the stock continued to drop. You can see from the numbers above that my total cost and money at risk was $230.63.

The stock had reported higher than expected Q4 earnings but had projected less than expected user growth. Three analysts had downgraded the stock. The trading volume was huge, well over 12 million shares traded. Average volume was a little over 2.2 million.

I thought the market had overreacted. I expected some type of bounce up the next week. The option expires Feb 20, 2015 which gave me a little over 2 weeks to see some type of comeback.

Research for the trade was about 20 minutes. All free on the Yahoo finance site.

On Monday, Feb 9, 2015 Yelp dropped another $3.00. Not what I had expected. My option was now worth about $60.00.

I still felt that the stock would recover so I decided to wait. Not a comfortable wait for me. Usually on a losing trade I try to get out with at least half of my original investment. Too late for that at this point. I could take a big loss or wait it out.

For the next 3 days the stock started to go back up and perform as I had anticipated. On Friday, Feb 13, 2015 the stock went to $49.00 at one point. I placed an order to sell and it filled fairly quickly.

With only 1 week remaining until the option expired I didn't want to risk holding. 14.616% return in 8 days is not bad.

RDWR- January 28, 2015

Date:	Activity	Qnty/Symbol	Description		Price	Fees	Amount
1-28-15	Bot to Open	1 RDWR call	Feb 20	20.00 call	$0.40	5.63	$45.63
2-04-15	Sold to Close	1 RDWR call	Feb 20	20.00 call	$0.55	5.65	$49.35

Money at risk: $45.63   Net gain: $3.72   Rate of Return: 8.152% in 8 days

ANNUAL RATE OF RETURN: 366.84%

Low risk trade with minimal gain.

All markets down big today. I found RDWR on the Yahoo loser list. I was not familiar with the stock. The stock was at $19.33, down $3.06. The company topped the 4Q forecasts but issued weaker than expected 1st quarter guidance.

I spent about 15 minutes checking the stock history, options, news.

I bid for a Feb 20 call for .40. The bid ask at the time was .30/.45. It took about 10 minutes before it filled.

My total capital invested and at risk is $45.63.

The drop seemed an overreaction to me and the lower price was also assisted with all the markets being down today.

My expectation is that the stock will recover somewhat and that I will see a profit on the transaction.

Well, it took about 8 days for the stock to get high enough for me to see a profit. As you can see from the numbers above it was a small gain. I didn't want to wait the additional 16 days until the option expired. As it was, the stock went higher for the next few days.

TZOO- January 22, 2015

Date:	Activity	Qnty/Symbol	Description		Price	Fees	Amount
1-22-15	Bot to Open	1 TZOO call	Feb 20	10.00 call	$0.35	5.63	$40.63
2-17-15	Sold to Close	1 TZOO call	Feb 20	10.00 call	$0.25	5.65	$19.35

Money at risk: $40.63   Net loss: ($21.28)   Rate of Return: (52.375%) in 27 days

Probably my largest percentage loss in awhile. Fortunately the dollar amount was small.

The market had a monster up day. The S&P, Dow and Nasdaq each were all up more than 1.5%.

Late in the day I found TZOO in one of my stock portfolios. I hadn't looked at it or played it for years. The stock had announced earnings that apparently weren't as high as expected. Earlier in the day the stock had hit its 52 week low at $9.53. The stock was $9.61 when I bid for a Feb 10 call for .35. The bid/ask at the time was .25/.40.

It filled within 10 minutes. My total cost was $40.63. This was my total money at risk.

The stock seemed to be stabilizing at the $9.60 mark. This was an interesting play for me. I would have preferred for the total market to be down and TZOO to be near its 52 week low. Often when the market has a great up day then some profit taking occurs the next day.

However, the three points that decided this play for me were: the stock was near its 52 week low, stock seemed to stabilize with less than one hour prior to market close, and the total cost of less than $41.00 was well within my budget.

I have until February 20, 2015 to realize a profit.

Obviously the stock didn't do as I had expected. It never bounced back up and I was lucky to get back almost half of my capital. I didn't feel horrible about this. Although I lost over 52% on the trade my net loss was less than $22.00.

Check my report titled, "How to Play a Losing Stock Option Trade". You can get it at www.amazon.com . Just type in my name, Hugh McDowell.

MTZ- January 16, 2015

Date:	Activity	Qnty/Symbol	Description		Price	Fees	Amount
1-16-15	Bot to Open	1 MTZ call	Feb 20	19.00 call	$1.00	5.63	$105.63
1-26-15	Sold to Close	1 MTZ call	Feb 20	19.00 call	$1.25	5.65	$119.35

Money at risk: $105.63   Net gain: $13.72   Rate of Return: 12.988% in 11 days

ANNUAL RATE OF RETURN: 428.604%

This was a low risk, decent gain trade.

Today all the markets (Dow, S&P, Nasdaq) were in positive territory. The gains were less than 1% higher than yesterday.

I checked the market about one and a half hours before close. Hadn't looked at it all day but had a couple of hours and feeling the urge to play. I found MTZ in one of my stock portfolios. These are lists of stocks that I have looked at and/or played over the years. I honestly don't remember ever playing this stock.

The stock price was $18.49, down 37 cents. Not a huge drop but near its 52 week low price of $18.14. I checked the historical price tab. For the last few years the stock has gone higher from January to February.

I placed a bid for a Feb 19 call for $1.00. The bid/ask at the time was .90/1.10. The bid filled immediately. My expectation was that prior to the Feb 20 expiration date the stock would go high enough for me to see a profit.

I spent a total of 20 minutes research which included placing the bid. Not a huge time commitment or capital outlay.

The stock price stayed flat for the next several days and there was no chance for a profit. On Jan 23, 2015 the price started to rise. This was a Friday. On Monday, January 26, 2015 the MTZ opened at $19.84. Since I wouldn't be able to watch the market that day, I sold early in the morning for a tidy 12.988 % return.

FCX- January 14, 2015

Date:	Activity	Qnty/Symbol	Description		Price	Fees	Amount
1-14-15	Bot to Open	1 FCX call	Feb 20	19.00 call	$1.18	5.63	$123.63
1-16-15	Sold to Close	1 FCX call	Feb 20	19.00 call	$1.33	5.65	$127.35

Money at risk: $123.63   Net gain: $3.72   Rate of Return: 3.008% in 3 days

ANNUAL RATE OF RETURN: 363.968%

My early exit on this trade was a mistake.

Market down today. Yesterday FCX was $21.04, down $1.72. Near its 52 week low. A mineral asset company, it had dropped because copper was near a 5 year low. Today when I checked the stock had dropped another $2.31, down to $18.73.

I didn't see any news specific to FCX, it seemed to be dropping in sympathy with the mineral sector.

A bit less than 90 minutes into the trading day, I bid for a Feb 19 call at $1.18. The bid/ask at the time was 1.13/1.23. It filled immediately. The stock is near a 6 year low and I don't expect it to fall much further.

The option expires February 20, 2015. That gives me 38 days to see some type of recovery. I originally found the stock on the Yahoo loser list.

Counting yesterday, my total research time was about 30 minutes.

I also made a play on another stock, ECOM today. The information for ECOM is explained next on my stock list.

On both stocks I expect some recovery in time for me to see a profit.

Two days later on Friday, January 16, 2015 FCX went up about 75 cents. I decided to sell for a small profit. Usually I don't like to hold a position over the weekend.

As it turned out, on the February expiration date (Feb 20, 2015) the stock ended the day at $21.28. I could have sold the option for at least $225.00. Substantially more than what I did sell it for.

I just couldn't hold it that long. I trade for fun and profit. Waiting that late would have stressed me out and not been fun. Plus, there was always the chance the stock could have dropped.

ECOM- January 14, 2015

Date:	Activity	Qnty/Symbol	Description		Price	Fees	Amount
1-14-15	Bot to Open	1 ECOM call	Mar 20	10.00 call	$1.00	5.63	$105.63
1-26-15	Sold to Close	1 ECOM call	Mar 20	10.00 call	$1.15	5.65	$109.35

Money at risk: $105.63   Net gain: $3.72   Rate of Return: 3.521% in 13 days

ANNUAL RATE OF RETURN: 98.868%

This was a ho-hum trade that should have done better.

As I mentioned in the FCX description, the markets were down today. I felt like playing. I found ECOM on the Yahoo loser list. The stock had dropped 65 cents, only 15 cents from its 52 week low. Stock price was $9.18. The 1 year target was $23.00.

I actually looked at the stock yesterday when it dropped from $21.15 to $9.83. Not sure why I didn't place a bid then. I wasn't real familiar with the stock. Total time researching the stock for both days was about 25 minutes.

The stock had plummeted due to 4Q (4th Quarter) revenue warning. Today the stock price seemed to stabilize around $9.18. About two and a half hours into the trading day.

My expectation was that the stock would start to recover. To give myself some leeway I placed a bid for a Mar 10 call. That gave me 66 days until the option expired.

I placed a bid for $1.00. The bid/ask at the time was .90/1.30. It filled quickly.

Monday, January 26, 2015

Almost two weeks and the stock just isn't performing like I had hoped it would. Today I decided to sell for a small profit.

I'd rather take back my capital and trade something with more potential.

Later I saw that ECOM had gone as high as $11.68. This was in the last two days prior to the option expiring. Had I waited that long I would have made a little more. But that was far more risk than I was willing to take. Seldom do I keep an option with only a couple of days remaining until expiration.

I've written an eBook on trading for fun and profit. That would not be fun for me, too much stress. You can find the book at www.amazon.com. The title is "How to Play the Market for Fun and Profit". Just type in the title or my name, Hugh McDowell and the book will pop up.

NES- January 12, 2015

Date:	Activity	Qnty/Symbol	Description		Price	Fees	Amount
1-12-15	Bot to Open	100 NES	NES	100 shares	$3.08	4.95	$312.95
1-13-15	Sold to Close	100 NES	NES	100 shares	$3.25	4.98	$320.02

Money at risk: $312.95   Net gain: $7.07   Rate of Return: 2.259% in 2 days

ANNUAL RATE OF RETURN: 411.138%

This was to be a short term covered call play but did not pan out.

Monday, January 12, 2015

Markets opened in negative territory and continued to drop. I found NES on the Yahoo loser list. I had never seen the stock before. I spent about 20 minutes checking it out.

The stock was $3.08, down $1.21. It had hit a 52 week low on no real negative news. The stock is in the Waste Management Industry and provides environmental solutions for oil and natural gas.

I think it is a victim of the oil industry woes. I usually don't play oil or oil related stocks. Too volatile and I just haven't had much luck in the past.

The stock does sell options but I decided to buy 100 shares for a potential covered call play. I bought the 100 shares for a total cost of $312.95.

I then placed a sell order for a Jan 2.50 call for 90 cents. This is really short term as the option expires in four days. If it is exercised I will make a small profit as well as have all my capital back to trade again.

The sell offer is good for today only. I like many aspects of this trade. I don't expect the call option to sell but do expect the stock to gain some momentum this week or next.

The option was never exercised that day so I had 100 shares in my account.

Tuesday, January 13, 2015

The markets opened up in positive territory.

About one and a half hours into the trading day I sold the 100 shares for a small profit. I wasn't getting a good feeling about the stock and wanted to free the capital for more trading.

Oil based stocks seem to be stalled. Since I already own 100 shares of another oil related stock (SZYM) I don't want to keep both. You can see the results of my SZYM trade later in this report.

I'm not thrilled with the results but any profit is better than a loss. And the annual return rate is nothing to be sneezed at.

SPHS- December 15, 2014

Date:	Activity	Qnty/Symbol	Description	Price	Fees	Amount
12-15-14	Bot to Open	100 SPHS	SPHS 100 shares	$0.50	4.95	$54.95
2-27-15	Sold to Close	100 SPHS	SPHS 100 shares	$0.7011	4.98	$65.13

Money at risk: $54.95   Net gain: $10.18   Rate of Return: 18.525% in 75 days

ANNUAL RATE OF RETURN: 74.1%

A rare trade in the biopharmaceutical sector that was profitable but not well suited to my trading style.

Monday, December 15, 2014

The markets were fairly flat today.

I found SPHS on the Yahoo loser list. The stock had an over 80% drop from Friday on a failed interim trial report. On Monday the stock had been $2.82. Today the price was around 50 cents.

I usually steer clear of biopharma companies. Especially during trial phases. I don't know much about them and they seem to be risky. And SPHS doesn't sell options.

However, the one year target was still $3.60. I thought I would buy 100 shares with the hope that the stock would pop up enough for me to see a profit.

I didn't see a lot more downside for the stock at this price. I bid .50 for 100 shares. The bid/ask at the time was .48/.52.

For less than $55.00 it was a low risk play.

Friday, February 27, 2015

For the last month and a half SPHS was flat. Not until today did it go high enough for me to sell the 100 shares for a small profit.

I made a decent rate of return but it took me 75 days. I really felt that the stock would have popped up sooner.

I could have held on to the stock for longer. But I like the thrill of testing and challenging the market. If I had to wait that long between trades I would go nuts!

SZYM- January 7, 2015

Date:	Activity	Qnty/Symbol	Description		Price	Fees	Amount
1-07-15	Bot to Open	100 SZYM	SZYM	100 shares	$2.23	4.95	$227.95
1-23-15	Sold to Open	1SZYM call	Feb 20	2.50 call	$0.20	5.65	$14.35
2-20-15	Assigned	1SZYM call	Feb 20	2.50 call			
2-20-15	Sold to Close	100 SPHS	SZYM	100 shares	$2.50	4.97	$245.03

Money at risk: $227.95   Net gain: $31.43   Rate of Return: 13.788% in 45 days

ANNUAL RATE OF RETURN: 110.304%

This is a good example of how a covered call play should work. Better suited for more conservative investors.

Wednesday, January 7, 2015

I found this stock from an online newsletter I receive. You may have heard of the Motley Fool. They were really touting this stock as high risk but a possible triple bagger. I don't even remember what the markets were doing that day.

I liked that the stock was a renewable plant based energy company. I thought I would buy 100 shares and sell a covered call on it. I bought the stock and waited for it to go up before selling a covered call. I originally wanted to sell a January call but the premiums were too low.

On January 23 the stock had gone up enough to sell a February covered call. I sold it for 20 cents. Not much, but I wanted to get a premium before I sold the stock.

On the February options expiration day, the stock was higher than $2.50 so my stock sold and I made the profit you see above.

This is not a bad rate of return with very low risk. I owned 100 shares and if the stock hadn't been bought I would have sold another covered call on it. But for me, it ties up my money for too long. I like matching wits with the market and when I play I want to have things happen quickly.

For those of you who are more conservative, selling covered calls on stock you own is a viable strategy. Check out my reports at www.amazon.com titled "Covered Call Play: How To Potentially Make 31% Return In Four Months" or "Covered Call Play Part 2: How to Potentially Earn Over 43% Return in 7 Months". Both are specific trades I did that made those returns.

EXXI- December 1, 2014

Date:	Activity	Qnty/Symbol	Description		Price	Fees	Amount
12-01-14	Bot to Open	100 EXXI	EXXI	100 shares	$3.30	4.95	$334.95
12-02-14	Sold to Open	1 EXXI call	Dec 20	3.50 call	$0.55	5.65	$49.35
12-19-14	Option expires						
12-22-14	Sold to Open	1 EXXI call	Jan 17	3.50 call	$0.35	5.65	$29.35
1-06-15	Bot to Close	1 EXXI call	Jan 17	3.50 call	$0.05	0.03	$ 5.03
1-07-15	Sold to Close	100 EXXI	EXXI	100 shares	$2.7501	4.98	$270.03

Money at risk: $339.98   Net gain: $8.75   Rate of Return: 2.573% in 38 days

ANNUAL RATE OF RETURN: 23.157%

This is a play that didn't work out as well as I had planned. Too much money tied up for too long a period.

This is a different type of trade than most of the option trades listed in this report. This is a covered call play. Briefly, with a covered call play you must own the stock and then you sell a call option on the stock. Most option contracts are in 100 share amounts so you must own 100 shares of a stock to sell 1 covered call.

To learn more about this type of trade check out my reports, "Covered Call Play: How to Potentially Make 31% Return in Four Months" or "Covered Call Play Part 2: How to Potentially Earn Over 43% Return in Seven Months". Both are at www.amazon.com. Just type in my name, Hugh McDowell and they will pop up.

This is a more conservative strategy for trading.

Monday, Dec 1, 2014

Markets were all slightly negative. I found EXXI on the Yahoo loser list but was familiar with the stock as I had traded it before. EXXI is an oil company that has been hammered by the worldwide oil glut.

The stock hit its 52 week low today. The 52 week target is listed at $15.92. When I saw it the stock price was $3.30.

I decided to buy 100 shares a $3.30. My total cost is $334.95. I want to sell a covered call on the stock. Oil stock should have a bounce up the next few days.

If the stock price continues to drop I should be able to get out without too much loss.

Tuesday, December 2, 2014

The markets are all up today and in positive territory. EXXI popped up to $3.70. A little less than two hours into the trading day I sold a covered call for 55 cents.

If the call option is exercised on December 19th, I will net a profit of $64.40. That means the stock will sell for $350. Subtract the costs and add the premium for a return of 19.226%.

This didn't happen. The stock dropped and never reached $3.50 by December 19th.

I then sold another covered call option on December 22nd for 35 cents. I then bought back my covered call option on January 6, 2015 for $5.03.

I thought the stock might pop higher in January but it stayed flat.

The next day I just sold the stock to get out of the trade completely. I made a very small profit but felt I could make more profitable trades with the capital.

On an annual basis this is not a bad rate of return but too little and too much time for a trading fool like me!

FINL- December 19, 2014

Date:	Activity	Qnty/Symbol	Description		Price	Fees	Amount
12-19-14	Bot to Open	1 FINL call	Jan 17	22.50 call	$0.95	5.63	$100.63
12-23-14	Sold to Close	1 FINL call	Jan 17	22.50 call	$1.10	5.65	$104.35

Money at risk: $100.63   Net gain: $3.72   Rate of Return: 3.696% in 5 days

ANNUAL RATE OF RETURN: 269.808%

A simple option trade that never realized its potential.

Friday, December 19, 2014

Two and a half hours into the day, the markets were flat. I found FINL on the Yahoo loser list. The stock price was $22.64, down $6.26. The company reported earnings that disappointed the market. The stock had its 52 week low in the first two hours of the trading day.

The trading volume was huge, by the end of the day over 7.3 million shares traded.

I watched the stock for about 20 minutes. It seemed to stabilize near its 52 week low.

I thought the selloff was a huge overreaction and expect some sort of bounce up next week. I place a bid for a January 22.50 call for .95. The bid/ask was .90/1.00. My order filled immediately.

This was a new stock for me. I had never seen or played it before.

Tuesday, December 23, 2014

For the next several days, FINL was flat. I decided to get out with a small profit and look elsewhere for a trade. Not a huge investment nor a large gain.

NTES- December 8, 2014

Date:	Activity	Qnty/Symbol	Description			Price	Fees	Amount
12-08-14	Bot to Open	1 NTES call	Dec 20	97.50 call		$2.20	5.63	$225.63
12-10-14	Sold to Close	1 NTES call	Dec 20	97.50 call		$3.30	5.65	$324.35

Money at risk: $225.63   Net gain: $98.72   Rate of Return: 43.753% in 3 days

ANNUAL RATE OF RETURN: 5,294.113%

CRUS- December 1, 2014

Date:	Activity	Qnty/Symbol	Description		Price	Fees	Amount
12-01-14	Bot to Open	1 CRUS call	Dec 20	17.50 call	$0.75	5.63	$80.63
12-04-14	Sold to Close	1 CRUS call	Dec 20	17.50 call	$0.60	5.65	$54.35

Money at risk: $80.63   Net loss: ($26.28)   Rate of Return: 32.593% in 4 days

AMRI- November 5, 2014

Date:	Activity	Qnty/Symbol	Description		Price	Fees	Amount
11-05-14	Bot to Open	1 AMRI call	Nov 22	17.50 call	$0.60	5.63	$65.63
11-21-14	Expired	1 AMRI call	Nov 22	17.50 call			

Money at risk: $65.63   Net loss: ($65.63)   Rate of Return: (100%) in 17 days

CRUS- October 31, 2014

Date:	Activity	Qnty/Symbol	Description		Price	Fees	Amount
10-31-14	Bot to Open	1 CRUS call	Nov 22	19.50 call	$0.55	5.63	$60.63

11-03-14   Sold to Close   1 CRUS call   Nov 22   19.50 call $0.75   5.65 $69.35

Money at risk: $60.63   Net gain: $8.72   Rate of Return: 14.382% in 4 days

ANNUAL RATE OF RETURN: 1,308.762%

EBAY- September 10, 2014

Date:	Activity	Qnty/Symbol	Description		Price	Fees	Amount
9-10-14	Bot to Open	1 EBAY call	Sep 20	51.50 call	$0.62	5.63	$67.63
9-11-14	Sold to Close	1 EBAY call	Sep 20	51.50 call	$0.40	5.65	$34.35

Money at risk: $67.63   Net loss: ($33.28)   Rate of Return: (49.208%) in 2 days

JAKK- July 24, 2014

Date:	Activity	Qnty/Symbol	Description		Price	Fees	Amount
7-24-14	Bot to Open	1 JAKK call	Aug 16	7.50 call	$0.25	5.64	$30.64
8-15-14	Expired	1 JAKK call	Aug 16	7.50 call			

Money at risk: $30.64   Net loss: ($30.64)   Rate of Return: (100%) in 23 days

SFUN- June 12, 2014

Date:	Activity	Qnty/Symbol	Description		Price	Fees	Amount
6-12-14	Bot to Open	1 SFUN call	Jun 19	9.00 call	$0.65	5.64	$70.64
6-18-14	Sold to Close	1 SFUN call	Jun 19	9.00 call	$0.85	5.66	$79.34

Money at risk: $70.64   Net gain: $8.70   Rate of Return: 12.315% in 7 days

ANNUAL RATE OF RETURN: 640.38%

FRAN- June 10, 2014

Date:	Activity	Qnty/Symbol	Description		Price	Fees	Amount
6-10-14	Bot to Open	1 FRAN call	Jun 19	12.50 call	$1.20	5.64	$125.64

6-11-14   Sold to Close   1 FRAN call   Jun 19   12.50 call $1.65   5.66 $159.34

Money at risk: $125.64   Net gain: $33.70   Rate of Return: 26.822% in 2 days

ANNUAL RATE OF RETURN: 4,881.604%

BLOX- June 3, 2014

Date:	Activity	Qnty/Symbol	Description		Price	Fees	Amount
6-03-14	Bot to Open	1 BLOX call	Jun 21	12.50 call	$0.70	5.64	$75.64
6-06-14	Sold to Close	1 BLOX call	Jun 21	12.50 call	$0.80	5.66	$74.34

Money at risk: $75.64   Net loss: ($1.30)   Rate of Return: (1.718%) in 4 days

INFN- February 28, 2014

Date:	Activity	Qnty/Symbol	Description		Price	Fees	Amount
2-28-14	Bot to Open	1 INFN call	Apr 19	8.00 call	$0.70	5.64	$75.64
3-04-14	Sold to Close	1INFN call	Apr 19	8.00 call	$0.85	5.66	$79.34

Money at risk: $75.64   Net gain: $3.70   Rate of Return: 4.891% in 5 days

ANNUAL RATE OF RETURN: 357.043%

GRPN- February 21, 2014

Date:	Activity	Qnty/Symbol	Description		Price	Fees	Amount
2-21-14	Bot to Open	1GRPN call	Mar 22	8.00 call	$0.67	5.66	$72.64
2-27-14	Sold to Close	1 GRPN call	Mar 22	8.00 call	$0.82	5.64	$76.34

Money at risk: $72.64   Net gain: $3.70   Rate of Return: 5.093% in 7 days

ANNUAL RATE OF RETURN: 264.836%

ANGI- February 14, 2014

Date:	Activity	Qnty/Symbol	Description	Price	Fees	Amount

| 2-14-14 | Bot to Open | 1 ANGI call | Mar 22 | 15.00 call | $1.10 | 5.64 | $115.64 |
| 2-19-14 | Sold to Close | 1 ANGI call | Mar 22 | 15.00 call | $0.75 | 5.66 | $69.34 |

Money at risk: $115.64   Net loss: ($46.30)   Rate of Return: (40.038%) in 6 days

MYGN- December 30, 2013

Date:	Activity	Qnty/Symbol	Description		Price	Fees	Amount
12-30-13	Bot to Open	1 MYGN call	Jan 18	20.00 call	$1.15	5.64	$120.64
12-31-13	Sold to Close	1 MYGN call	Jan 18	20.00 call	$1.30	5.66	$124.34

Money at risk: $120.64   Net gain: $3.70   Rate of Return: 3.066% in 2 days

ANNUAL RATE OF RETURN: 558.012%

JBL- December 18, 2013

Date:	Activity	Qnty/Symbol	Description		Price	Fees	Amount
12-18-13	Bot to Open	1 JBL call	Jan 18	16.00 call	$0.45	5.64	$50.64
12-23-13	Sold to Close	1 JBL call	Jan 18	16.00 call	$0.75	5.66	$69.34

Money at risk: $50.64   Net gain: $18.70   Rate of Return: 36.927% in 6 days

ANNUAL RATE OF RETURN: 2,215.62%

WU- November 14, 2013

Date:	Activity	Qnty/Symbol	Description	Price	Fees	Amount
11-14-13	Bot to Open	1 WU call	Dec 21 17.00 call	$0.70	5.64	$75.64
12-18-13	Sold to Close	1 WU call	Dec 21 17.00 call	$0.10	5.66	$4.34

Money at risk: $75.64   Net loss: ($71.30)   Rate of Return: (94.262%) in 35 days

INWK- November 7, 2013

Date:	Activity	Qnty/Symbol	Description	Price	Fees	Amount

| 11-07-13 | Bot to Open | 1 INWK call | Dec 21 | 5.00 call | $1.00 | 5.64 | $105.64 |
| 11-11-13 | Sold to Close | 1 INWK call | Dec 21 | 5.00 call | $1.15 | 5.66 | $109.34 |

Money at risk: $105.64   Net gain: $3.70   Rate of Return: 3.502% in 5 days

ANNUAL RATE OF RETURN: 255.646%

BSFT- November 5, 2013

Date:	Activity	Qnty/Symbol	Description		Price	Fees	Amount
11-05-13	Bot to Open	1 BSFT call	Nov 16	25.00 call	$1.05	5.64	$110.64
11-06-13	Sold to Close	1 BSFT call	Nov 16	25.00 call	$1.20	5.66	$114.34

Money at risk: $110.64   Net gain: $3.70   Rate of Return: 3.344% in 2 days

ANNUAL RATE OF RETURN: 608.608%

WU- October 30, 2013

Date:	Activity	Qnty/Symbol	Description		Price	Fees	Amount
10-30-13	Bot to Open	1 WU call	Nov 16	17.00 call	$0.35	5.64	$40.64
11-01-13	Sold to Close	1 WU call	Nov 16	17.00 call	$0.50	5.66	$44.34

Money at risk: $40.64   Net gain: $3.70   Rate of Return: 9.104% in 3 days

ANNUAL RATE OF RETURN: 1,101.584%

PIR- October 21, 2013

Date:	Activity	Qnty/Symbol	Description		Price	Fees	Amount
10-21-13	Bot to Open	1 PIR call	Nov 16	21.00 call	$0.45	5.64	$50.64
10-23-13	Sold to Close	1 PIR call	Nov 16	21.00 call	$0.60	5.66	$54.34

Money at risk: $50.64   Net gain: $3.70   Rate of Return: 7.306% in 3 days

ANNUAL RATE OF RETURN: 884.026%

TWGP- September 18, 2013

Date:	Activity	Qnty/Symbol	Description		Price	Fees	Amount
9-18-13	Bot to Open	1 TWGP call	Oct 19	10.00 call	$0.85	5.64	$90.64
9-19-13	Sold to Close	1 TWGP call	Oct 19	10.00 call	$1.20	5.66	$114.34

Money at risk: $90.64   Net gain: $23.70   Rate of Return: 26.147% in 2 days

ANNUAL RATE OF RETURN: 4,758.754%

CRUS- September 16, 2013

Date:	Activity	Qnty/Symbol	Description		Price	Fees	Amount
9-16-13	Bot to Open	1 CRUS call	Oct 19	22.00 call	$1.15	5.64	$120.64
9-17-13	Sold to Close	1 CRUS call	Oct 19	22.00 call	$1.35	5.66	$129.34

Money at risk: $120.64   Net gain: $8.70   Rate of Return: 7.211% in 2 days

ANNUAL RATE OF RETURN: 1,312.402%

SGI- August 8, 2013

Date:	Activity	Qnty/Symbol	Description		Price	Fees	Amount
8-08-13	Bot to Open	1 SGI call	Sep 21	15.00 call	$1.00	5.64	$105.64
8-13-13	Sold to Close	1 SGI call	Sep 21	15.00 call	$1.25	5.66	$119.34

Money at risk: $105.64   Net gain: $13.70   Rate of Return: 12.968% in 6 days

ANNUAL RATE OF RETURN: 778.08%

SYNA- August 5, 2013

Date:	Activity	Qnty/Symbol	Description		Price	Fees	Amount
8-05-13	Bot to Open	1 SYNA call	Aug 17	40.00 call	$0.75	5.64	$80.64
8-06-13	Sold to Close	1 SYNA call	Aug 17	40.00 call	$1.30	5.66	$124.34

Money at risk: $80.64   Net gain: $43.70   Rate of Return: 54.191% in 2 days

ANNUAL RATE OF RETURN: 9,862.762%

APOL- August 1, 2013

Date:	Activity	Qnty/Symbol	Description		Price	Fees	Amount
8-01-13	Bot to Open	1 APOL put	Aug 17	20.00 put	$1.05	5.64	$110.64
8-02-13	Sold to Close	1 APOL put	Aug 17	20.00 put	$0.93	5.66	$87.34

Money at risk: $110.64   Net loss: ($23.30)   Rate of Return: (21.059%) in 2 days

CPN-July 25, 2013

Date:	Activity	Qnty/Symbol	Description		Price	Fees	Amount
7-25-13	Bot to Open	1 CPN call	Aug 17	20.00 call	$0.25	5.64	$30.64
7-26-13	Sold to Close	1 CPN call	Aug 17	20.00 call	$0.40	5.66	$34.34

Money at risk: $30.64   Net gain: $3.70   Rate of Return: 12.075% in 2 days

ANNUAL RATE OF RETURN: 2,197.65%

There it is. That's it. Strategies from 50 actual trades that anyone can do.

Let me repeat. For additional strategies on my trading style, check me out at www.amazon.com. Type in my name, Hugh McDowell and the other books and reports that I've written on playing the market should come up. All are e-books and inexpensive.

Learn these strategies and adapt them to your own trading style. Paper trade for free until you feel comfortable making real trades.

Here's an additional bonus for you. I've written a report titled "Four Kick A$$ Trades in Eight Days". These were four trades I made while writing "Mad Diary" but was unable to put in that book. The trades were executed from April 28, 2015 – May 5, 2015.

This was one of the best eight day trading periods I have had in 15 years of trading. The returns were fantastic; 200.754% in two days, 128.094% in two days, 35.788% in four days and 12.413% in two days!

The stocks were all unknown to me prior to trading and I spent about two hours of research for all the trades. Not two hours per trade but two hours total.

Send me an email to hcmcdowell@hotmail.com and I will email it to you for free. Just put Diary in the subject line.

This is a limited time offer and will expire once I publish "Four Kick A$$ Trades in Eight Days" on Amazon. That will probably be in the next 2-3 weeks.

OOPS. Gotta' go. I hear the sound of the opening bell.

Happy Trading!!!